www.EffortlessMath.com

... So Much More Online!

✓ FREE Math lessons

✓ More Math learning books!

✓ Mathematics Worksheets

✓ Online Math Tutors

Need a PDF version of this book?

Visit www.EffortlessMath.com

5 Full Length SSAT Lower Level Math Practice Tests

The Practice You Need to Ace the SSAT

Lower Level Math Test

By

Reza Nazari & Ava Ross

All inquiries should be addressed to:

info@EffortlessMath.com

www.EffortlessMath.com

ISBN-13: 978-1-64612-116-8

ISBN-10: 1-64612-116-3

Published by: Effortless Math Education

www.EffortlessMath.com

Description

5 Full-Length SSAT Lower Level Math Practice Tests, which reflects the 2019 and 2020 test guidelines and topics, is designed to help you hone your math skills, overcome your exam anxiety, and boost your confidence -- and do your best to ace the SSAT Lower Level Math Test. The realistic and full-length SSAT Lower Level Math tests show you how the test is structured and what math topics you need to master. The practice test questions are followed by answer explanations to help you find your weak areas, learn from your mistakes, and raise your SSAT Lower Level Math score.

The surest way to succeed on SSAT Lower Level Math Test is with intensive practice in every math topic tested-- and that's what you will get in *5 Full-Length SSAT Lower Level Math Practice Tests*. This SSAT Lower Level Math new edition has been updated to replicate questions appearing on the most recent SSAT Lower Level Math tests. This is a precious learning tool for SSAT Lower Level test takers who need extra practice in math to improve their SSAT Lower Level Math score. After taking the SSAT Lower Level Math practice tests in this book, you will have solid foundation and adequate practice that is necessary to succeed on the SSAT Lower Level Math test. **This book is your ticket to ace the SSAT Lower Level Math Test!**

5 Full-Length SSAT Lower Level Math Practice Tests contains many exciting and unique features to help you improve your test scores, including:

- Content 100% aligned with the 2019 - 2020 SSAT Lower Level Math test

- Written by SSAT Math tutors and test experts

- Complete coverage of all SSAT Lower Level Math concepts and topics which you will be tested

- Detailed answers and explanations for every SSAT Lower Level Math practice questions to help you learn from your mistakes

- 5 full-length practice tests (featuring new question types) with detailed answers

This SSAT Lower Level Math book and other Effortless Math Education books are used by thousands of students each year to help them review core content areas, brush-up in math, discover their strengths and weaknesses, and achieve their best scores on the SSAT Lower Level Math test.

About the Author

Reza Nazari is the author of more than 100 Math learning books including:
– **Math and Critical Thinking Challenges:** For the Middle and High School Student
– **ACT Math in 30 Days.**
– **ASVAB Math Workbook 2018 – 2019**
– **Effortless Math Education Workbooks**
– **and many more Mathematics books …**

Reza is also an experienced Math instructor and a test–prep expert who has been tutoring students since 2008. Reza is the founder of Effortless Math Education, a tutoring company that has helped many students raise their standardized test scores—and attend the colleges of their dreams. Reza provides an individualized custom learning plan and the personalized attention that makes a difference in how students view math.

You can contact Reza via email at:
reza@EffortlessMath.com

Find Reza's professional profile at:
goo.gl/zoC9rJ

Contents

Description 4

SSAT Lower Level Math Practice Tests 7

SSAT Lower Level Math Practice Test 1 11

SSAT Lower Level Math Practice Test 2 19

SSAT Lower Level Math Practice Test 3 27

SSAT Lower Level Math Practice Test 4 35

SSAT Lower Level Math Practice Test 5 43

SSAT LOWER LEVEL Math Practice Tests Answer Keys 52

SSAT Lower Level Math Practice Tests Answers and Explanations 55

SSAT Lower Level Math Practice Tests

The SSAT, or Secondary School Admissions Test, is a standardized test to help determine admission to private elementary, middle and high schools.

There are currently three Levels of the SSAT:

- ✓ Lower Level (for students in 3rd and 4th grade)
- ✓ Middle Level (for students in 5th-7th grade)
- ✓ Upper Level (for students in 8th-11th grade)

There are four sections on the SSAT Lower Level Test:

- ✓ Quantitative (Mathematics) section: 30 questions, 30 minutes.
- ✓ Verbal section: 30 questions, 20 minutes.
- ✓ Reading section: 7 short passages, 28 questions, 30 minutes.
- ✓ Writing sample: 15 minutes to write a short passage

In this book, there are five complete SSAT Lower Level Quantitative practice tests. Take these tests to see what score you'll be able to receive on a real SSAT Lower Level test.

Good luck!

Time to refine your skill with a practice examination

Take a practice SSAT Lower Level Mathematics Test to simulate the test day experience. After you've finished, score your test using the answer key.

Before You Start

- You'll need a pencil and a timer to take the test.

- After you've finished the test, review the answer key to see where you went wrong.

- Use the answer sheet provided to record your answers. (You can cut it out or photocopy it)

- You will receive 1 point for every correct answer. You won't receive any point for wrong or skipped answers.

Calculators are NOT permitted for the SSAT Lower Level Test

Good Luck!

SSAT Lower Level Mathematics Practice Test Answer Sheet

Remove (or photocopy) this answer sheet and use it to complete the practice test.

SSAT Lower Level Mathematics Practice Test Answer Sheet

SSAT Lower Level Practice Test 1

1	Ⓐ Ⓑ Ⓒ Ⓓ Ⓔ	11	Ⓐ Ⓑ Ⓒ Ⓓ Ⓔ	21	Ⓐ Ⓑ Ⓒ Ⓓ Ⓔ
2	Ⓐ Ⓑ Ⓒ Ⓓ Ⓔ	12	Ⓐ Ⓑ Ⓒ Ⓓ Ⓔ	22	Ⓐ Ⓑ Ⓒ Ⓓ Ⓔ
3	Ⓐ Ⓑ Ⓒ Ⓓ Ⓔ	13	Ⓐ Ⓑ Ⓒ Ⓓ Ⓔ	23	Ⓐ Ⓑ Ⓒ Ⓓ Ⓔ
4	Ⓐ Ⓑ Ⓒ Ⓓ Ⓔ	14	Ⓐ Ⓑ Ⓒ Ⓓ Ⓔ	24	Ⓐ Ⓑ Ⓒ Ⓓ Ⓔ
5	Ⓐ Ⓑ Ⓒ Ⓓ Ⓔ	15	Ⓐ Ⓑ Ⓒ Ⓓ Ⓔ	25	Ⓐ Ⓑ Ⓒ Ⓓ Ⓔ
6	Ⓐ Ⓑ Ⓒ Ⓓ Ⓔ	16	Ⓐ Ⓑ Ⓒ Ⓓ Ⓔ	26	Ⓐ Ⓑ Ⓒ Ⓓ Ⓔ
7	Ⓐ Ⓑ Ⓒ Ⓓ Ⓔ	17	Ⓐ Ⓑ Ⓒ Ⓓ Ⓔ	27	Ⓐ Ⓑ Ⓒ Ⓓ Ⓔ
8	Ⓐ Ⓑ Ⓒ Ⓓ Ⓔ	18	Ⓐ Ⓑ Ⓒ Ⓓ Ⓔ	28	Ⓐ Ⓑ Ⓒ Ⓓ Ⓔ
9	Ⓐ Ⓑ Ⓒ Ⓓ Ⓔ	19	Ⓐ Ⓑ Ⓒ Ⓓ Ⓔ	29	Ⓐ Ⓑ Ⓒ Ⓓ Ⓔ
10	Ⓐ Ⓑ Ⓒ Ⓓ Ⓔ	20	Ⓐ Ⓑ Ⓒ Ⓓ Ⓔ	30	Ⓐ Ⓑ Ⓒ Ⓓ Ⓔ

Time to Test

Time to refine your skill with a practice examination

Take two practice SSAT Lower Level Mathematics Tests to simulate the test day experience. After you've finished, score your test using the answer key.

Before You Start

- You'll need a pencil and a timer to take the test.
- After you've finished the test, review the answer key to see where you went wrong.
- You will receive 1 point for every correct answer. You won't receive any point for wrong or skipped answers.
- Use the answer sheet provided to record your answers.

Calculators are NOT permitted for the SSAT Lower Level Test

Good Luck!

SSAT Lower Level Math Practice Test 1

2019 - 2020

Total number of questions: 30

Total time for this test: 30 Minutes

Calculator is NOT permitted for SSAT Lower Level Math Test.

SSAT Lower Level Mathematics Practice Test Answer Sheet

Remove (or photocopy) this answer sheet and use it to complete the practice test.

SSAT Lower Level Mathematics Practice Test Answer Sheet

SSAT Lower Level Practice Test 1

1	Ⓐ Ⓑ Ⓒ Ⓓ Ⓔ	11 Ⓐ Ⓑ Ⓒ Ⓓ Ⓔ	21 Ⓐ Ⓑ Ⓒ Ⓓ Ⓔ
2	Ⓐ Ⓑ Ⓒ Ⓓ Ⓔ	12 Ⓐ Ⓑ Ⓒ Ⓓ Ⓔ	22 Ⓐ Ⓑ Ⓒ Ⓓ Ⓔ
3	Ⓐ Ⓑ Ⓒ Ⓓ Ⓔ	13 Ⓐ Ⓑ Ⓒ Ⓓ Ⓔ	23 Ⓐ Ⓑ Ⓒ Ⓓ Ⓔ
4	Ⓐ Ⓑ Ⓒ Ⓓ Ⓔ	14 Ⓐ Ⓑ Ⓒ Ⓓ Ⓔ	24 Ⓐ Ⓑ Ⓒ Ⓓ Ⓔ
5	Ⓐ Ⓑ Ⓒ Ⓓ Ⓔ	15 Ⓐ Ⓑ Ⓒ Ⓓ Ⓔ	25 Ⓐ Ⓑ Ⓒ Ⓓ Ⓔ
6	Ⓐ Ⓑ Ⓒ Ⓓ Ⓔ	16 Ⓐ Ⓑ Ⓒ Ⓓ Ⓔ	26 Ⓐ Ⓑ Ⓒ Ⓓ Ⓔ
7	Ⓐ Ⓑ Ⓒ Ⓓ Ⓔ	17 Ⓐ Ⓑ Ⓒ Ⓓ Ⓔ	27 Ⓐ Ⓑ Ⓒ Ⓓ Ⓔ
8	Ⓐ Ⓑ Ⓒ Ⓓ Ⓔ	18 Ⓐ Ⓑ Ⓒ Ⓓ Ⓔ	28 Ⓐ Ⓑ Ⓒ Ⓓ Ⓔ
9	Ⓐ Ⓑ Ⓒ Ⓓ Ⓔ	19 Ⓐ Ⓑ Ⓒ Ⓓ Ⓔ	29 Ⓐ Ⓑ Ⓒ Ⓓ Ⓔ
10	Ⓐ Ⓑ Ⓒ Ⓓ Ⓔ	20 Ⓐ Ⓑ Ⓒ Ⓓ Ⓔ	30 Ⓐ Ⓑ Ⓒ Ⓓ Ⓔ

1. In the following figure, the shaded squares are what fractional part of the whole set of squares?

    A) $\frac{1}{2}$

    B) $\frac{5}{8}$

    C) $\frac{2}{3}$

    D) $\frac{3}{5}$

    E) $\frac{6}{11}$

      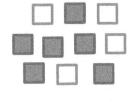

2. Which of the following is greater than $\frac{12}{8}$?

    A) $\frac{1}{2}$

    B) $\frac{5}{2}$

    C) $\frac{3}{4}$

    D) 1

    E) 1.4

3. If $\frac{1}{3}$ of a number is greater than 8, the number must be .....

    A) Less than 4

    B) Equal to 16

    C) Equal to 24

    D) Greater than 24

    E) Equal to 32

4. If $4 \times (M + N) = 20$ and M is greater than 0, then N could Not be .....

    A) 1

    B) 2

    C) 3

    D) 4

    E) 5

5. Which of the following is closest to 5.03?

    A) 6

    B) 5.5

    C) 5

    D) 5.4

    E) 6.5

6. At a Zoo, the ratio of lions to tigers is 10 to 6. Which of the following could NOT be the total number of lions and tigers in the zoo?
   A) 64
   B) 80
   C) 98
   D) 104
   E) 160

7. In the multiplication bellow, A represents which digit?
$$14 \times 3A2 = 4,788$$
   A) 2
   B) 3
   C) 4
   D) 6
   E) 8

8. If N is an even number, which of the following is always an odd number?
   A) $\dfrac{N}{2}$
   B) $N + 4$
   C) $2N$
   D) $(2 \times N) + 2$
   E) $N + 1$

9. $8.9 - 4.08$ is closest to which of the following.
   A) 4.1
   B) 4.8
   C) 6
   D) 8
   E) 13

$$x = 2,456 \qquad y = 259$$

10. Numbers x and y are shown above. How many times larger is the value of digit 5 in the number x, than the value of digit 5 in the number y?
    A) 1
    B) 10
    C) 100
    D) 1,000
    E) 10,000

11. If 5 added to a number, the sum is 20. If the same number added to 25, the answer is
    A) 30
    B) 35
    C) 40
    D) 45
    E) 50

12. $\dfrac{2+5+6\times1+1}{3+5}=?$
    A) $\dfrac{15}{8}$
    B) $\dfrac{4}{8}$
    C) $\dfrac{7}{4}$
    D) $\dfrac{6}{8}$
    E) $\dfrac{10}{8}$

13. What is the Area of the square shown in the following square?
    A) 2
    B) 4
    C) 6
    D) 8
    E) 10

14. If 20 is the product of 4 and x, then 20 can be divided by which of the following?
    A) $x + 4$
    B) $2x - 4$
    C) $x - 2$
    D) $x \times 4$
    E) $x + 1$

15. Use the equations below to answer the question:
$$x + 12 = 18$$
$$16 + y = 21$$

What is the value of $x + y$?

    A) 9
    B) 10
    C) 11
    D) 12
    E) 14

16. Which of the following expressions has the same value as $\frac{5}{4} \times \frac{6}{2}$?
    A) $\frac{6 \times 3}{4}$
    B) $\frac{6 \times 2}{4}$
    C) $\frac{5 \times 6}{4}$
    D) $\frac{5 \times 3}{4}$
    E) $\frac{8 \times 3}{4}$

17. When 5 is added to three times number N, the result is 41. Then N is ….
    A) 11
    B) 12
    C) 14
    D) 16
    E) 18

18. At noon, the temperature was 15 degrees. By midnight, it had dropped another 20 degrees. What was the temperature at midnight?
    A) 10 degrees above zero
    B) 10 degrees below zero
    C) 5 degrees above zero
    D) 5 degrees below zero
    E) 15 degrees below zero

19. If a triangle has a base of 5 cm and a height of 8 cm, what is the area of the triangle?
    A) $15cm^2$
    B) $20cm^2$
    C) $40cm^2$
    D) $45cm^2$
    E) $50cm^2$

20. Which formula would you use to find the area of a square?
    A) $length \times width \times height$
    B) $\frac{1}{2} base \times height$
    C) $length \times width$
    D) $side \times side$
    E) $\frac{1}{2}(length \times width \times heigt)$

21. What is the next number in this sequence?   2, 5, 9, 14, 20, ...
    A) 27
    B) 26
    C) 25
    D) 21
    E) 20

22. What is the average of the following numbers?   6, 10, 12, 23, 45
    A) 19
    B) 19.2
    C) 19.5
    D) 20
    E) 25

23. If there are 8 red balls and 12 blue balls in a basket, what is the probability that John will pick out a red ball from the basket?
    A) $\frac{18}{10}$
    B) $\frac{2}{5}$
    C) $\frac{2}{10}$
    D) $\frac{3}{5}$
    E) $\frac{20}{10}$

24. How many lines of symmetry does an equilateral triangle have?
    A) 5
    B) 4
    C) 3
    D) 2
    E) 1

25. What is 10% of 200?
    A) 10
    B) 20
    C) 30
    D) 40
    E) 50

26. Which of the following statement is False?
    A) $2 \times 2 = 4$
    B) $(4 + 1) \times 5 = 25$
    C) $6 \div (3 - 1) = 1$
    D) $6 \times (4 - 2) = 12$
    E) $(10 + 23) \times 10 = 330$

27. If all the sides in the following figure are of equal length and length of one side is 4, what is the perimeter of the figure?
    A) 15
    B) 18
    C) 20
    D) 24
    E) 28

28. $\frac{4}{5} - \frac{3}{5} = ?$
    A) 0.3
    B) 0.35
    C) 0.2
    D) 0.25
    E) 0.1

29. If $N = 2$ and $\frac{64}{N} + 4 = \square$, then $\square = \ldots$
    A) 30
    B) 32
    C) 34
    D) 36
    E) 38

30. Four people can paint 4 houses in 10 days. How many people are needed to paint 8 houses in 5 days?
    A) 6
    B) 8
    C) 12
    D) 16
    E) 20

End of SSAT Lower Level Math Practice Test 1

SSAT Lower Level Math Practice Test 2

2019 - 2020

Total number of questions: 30

Total time for this test: 30 Minutes

Calculator is NOT permitted for SSAT Lower Level Math Test.

SSAT Lower Level Mathematics Practice Test Answer Sheet

Remove (or photocopy) this answer sheet and use it to complete the practice test.

SSAT Lower Level Mathematics Practice Test Answer Sheet

SSAT Lower Level Practice Test 2

1	Ⓐ Ⓑ Ⓒ Ⓓ Ⓔ	11 Ⓐ Ⓑ Ⓒ Ⓓ Ⓔ	21 Ⓐ Ⓑ Ⓒ Ⓓ Ⓔ	
2	Ⓐ Ⓑ Ⓒ Ⓓ Ⓔ	12 Ⓐ Ⓑ Ⓒ Ⓓ Ⓔ	22 Ⓐ Ⓑ Ⓒ Ⓓ Ⓔ	
3	Ⓐ Ⓑ Ⓒ Ⓓ Ⓔ	13 Ⓐ Ⓑ Ⓒ Ⓓ Ⓔ	23 Ⓐ Ⓑ Ⓒ Ⓓ Ⓔ	
4	Ⓐ Ⓑ Ⓒ Ⓓ Ⓔ	14 Ⓐ Ⓑ Ⓒ Ⓓ Ⓔ	24 Ⓐ Ⓑ Ⓒ Ⓓ Ⓔ	
5	Ⓐ Ⓑ Ⓒ Ⓓ Ⓔ	15 Ⓐ Ⓑ Ⓒ Ⓓ Ⓔ	25 Ⓐ Ⓑ Ⓒ Ⓓ Ⓔ	
6	Ⓐ Ⓑ Ⓒ Ⓓ Ⓔ	16 Ⓐ Ⓑ Ⓒ Ⓓ Ⓔ	26 Ⓐ Ⓑ Ⓒ Ⓓ Ⓔ	
7	Ⓐ Ⓑ Ⓒ Ⓓ Ⓔ	17 Ⓐ Ⓑ Ⓒ Ⓓ Ⓔ	27 Ⓐ Ⓑ Ⓒ Ⓓ Ⓔ	
8	Ⓐ Ⓑ Ⓒ Ⓓ Ⓔ	18 Ⓐ Ⓑ Ⓒ Ⓓ Ⓔ	28 Ⓐ Ⓑ Ⓒ Ⓓ Ⓔ	
9	Ⓐ Ⓑ Ⓒ Ⓓ Ⓔ	19 Ⓐ Ⓑ Ⓒ Ⓓ Ⓔ	29 Ⓐ Ⓑ Ⓒ Ⓓ Ⓔ	
10	Ⓐ Ⓑ Ⓒ Ⓓ Ⓔ	20 Ⓐ Ⓑ Ⓒ Ⓓ Ⓔ	30 Ⓐ Ⓑ Ⓒ Ⓓ Ⓔ	

1. $\frac{8}{2} - \frac{3}{2} = ?$
   A) 1
   B) 1.5
   C) 2
   D) 2.5
   E) 3

2. If $48 = 3 \times N + 12$, then $N = \ldots$
   A) 8
   B) 12
   C) 14
   D) 15
   E) 20

3. The area of each square in the following shape is $8\ cm^2$. What is the area of shaded squares?
   A) $40\ cm^2$
   B) $42 cm^2$
   C) $44 cm^2$
   D) $45 cm^2$
   E) $46 cm^2$

4. What is the value of x in the following math equation?
   $$\frac{x}{15} + 9 = 11$$
   A) 15
   B) 20
   C) 25
   D) 28
   E) 30

5. When 3 is added to four times a number N, the result is 23. Which of the following equations represents this statement?
   A) $4 + 3N = 23$
   B) $23N + 4 = 3$
   C) $4N + 3 = 23$
   D) $4N + 23 = 3$
   E) $3N + 23 = 4$

6. When 78 is divided by 5, the remainder is the same as when 45 is divided by
   A) 2
   B) 4
   C) 5
   D) 7
   E) 9

7. John has 2,400 cards and Max has 606 cards. How many more cards does John have than Max?
   A) 1,794
   B) 1,798
   C) 1,812
   D) 1,828
   E) 1,994

8. In the following right triangle, what is the value of x?
   A) 15
   B) 30
   C) 45
   D) 60
   E) It cannot be determined from the information given

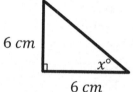

9. What is 5 percent of 480?
   A) 20
   B) 24
   C) 30
   D) 40
   E) 44

10. In a basket, the ratio of red marbles to blue marbles is 3 to 2. Which of the following could NOT be the total number of red and blue marbles in the basket?
   A) 15
   B) 32
   C) 55
   D) 60
   E) 70

11. A square has an area of 81 cm^2. What is its perimeter?
   A) 28 cm
   B) 32 cm
   C) 34 cm
   D) 36 cm
   E) 54 cm

12. Find the missing number in the sequence? $5, 8, 12, \ldots, 23$
   A) 15
   B) 17
   C) 18
   D) 20
   E) 22

13. The length of a rectangle is 3 times of its width. If the length is 18, what is the perimeter of the rectangle?
   A) 24
   B) 30
   C) 36
   D) 48
   E) 56

14. Mary has y dollars. John has $10 more than Mary. If John gives Mary $12, then in terms of y, how much does John have now?
   A) $y + 1$
   B) $y + 10$
   C) $y - 2$
   D) $y - 1$
   E) $y + 3$

15. Dividing 107 by 6 leaves a remainder of
   A) 1
   B) 2
   C) 3
   D) 4
   E) 5

16. If $6,000 + A - 200 = 7,400$, then $A =$
   A) 200
   B) 600
   C) 1,600
   D) 2,200
   E) 3,000

17. For what price is 15 percent off the same as $75 off?
   A) $200
   B) $300
   C) $350
   D) $400
   E) $500

18. Which of the following numbers is less than $\frac{3}{2}$?
    A) 1.4
    B) $\frac{5}{2}$
    C) 2.8
    D) 3
    E) 3.2

19. Use the equation below to answer the question.
$$x + 3 = 6$$
$$2y = 8$$
    What is the value of $y - x$?
    A) 1
    B) 2
    C) 3
    D) 4
    E) 5

20. If $310 - x + 116 = 225$, then $x =$
    A) 101
    B) 156
    C) 201
    D) 211
    E) 310

21. Of the following, 25 percent of $43.99 is closest to
    A) $9.90
    B) $10.00
    C) $11.00
    D) $11.50
    E) $12.00

22. Solve.
    $8.08 - 5.6 = ...$
    A) 2.42
    B) 2.46
    C) 2.48
    D) 3
    E) 3.2

23. If $500 + \square - 180 = 1,100$, then $\square = ?$
    A) 580
    B) 660
    C) 700
    D) 780
    E) 900

24. There are 60 students in a class. If the ratio of the number of girls to the total number of students in the class is $\frac{1}{6}$, which are the following is the number of boys in that class?
    A) 10
    B) 20
    C) 25
    D) 40
    E) 50

25. If $N \times (5 - 3) = 12$ then $N = ?$
    A) 6
    B) 12
    C) 13
    D) 14
    E) 18

26. If $x \blacksquare y = 3x + y - 2$, what is the value of $4 \blacksquare 12$?
    A) 4
    B) 18
    C) 22
    D) 36
    E) 48

27. Of the following, which number if the greatest?
    A) 0.092
    B) 0.8913
    C) 0.8923
    D) 0.8896
    E) 0.88

28. $\frac{7}{8} - \frac{3}{4} =$
    A) 0.125
    B) 0.375
    C) 0.5
    D) 0.625
    E) 0.775

29. Which of the following is the closest to 4.02?
    A) 4
    B) 4.2
    C) 4.3
    D) 4.4
    E) 4.5

30. Which of the following statements is False?
    A) $(7 \times 2 + 14) \times 2 = 56$
    B) $(2 \times 5 + 4) \div 2 = 7$
    C) $3 + (3 \times 6) = 21$
    D) $4 \times (3 + 9) = 48$
    E) $14 \div (2 + 5) = 5$

End of SSAT Lower Level Math Practice Test 2

SSAT Lower Level Math Practice Test 3

2019 - 2020

Total number of questions: 30

Total time for this test: 30 Minutes

Calculator is NOT permitted for SSAT Lower Level Math Test.

SSAT Lower Level Mathematics Practice Test Answer Sheet

Remove (or photocopy) this answer sheet and use it to complete the practice test.

SSAT Lower Level Mathematics Practice Test Answer Sheet

SSAT Lower Level Practice Test 3

1	Ⓐ Ⓑ Ⓒ Ⓓ Ⓔ	11	Ⓐ Ⓑ Ⓒ Ⓓ Ⓔ	21	Ⓐ Ⓑ Ⓒ Ⓓ Ⓔ
2	Ⓐ Ⓑ Ⓒ Ⓓ Ⓔ	12	Ⓐ Ⓑ Ⓒ Ⓓ Ⓔ	22	Ⓐ Ⓑ Ⓒ Ⓓ Ⓔ
3	Ⓐ Ⓑ Ⓒ Ⓓ Ⓔ	13	Ⓐ Ⓑ Ⓒ Ⓓ Ⓔ	23	Ⓐ Ⓑ Ⓒ Ⓓ Ⓔ
4	Ⓐ Ⓑ Ⓒ Ⓓ Ⓔ	14	Ⓐ Ⓑ Ⓒ Ⓓ Ⓔ	24	Ⓐ Ⓑ Ⓒ Ⓓ Ⓔ
5	Ⓐ Ⓑ Ⓒ Ⓓ Ⓔ	15	Ⓐ Ⓑ Ⓒ Ⓓ Ⓔ	25	Ⓐ Ⓑ Ⓒ Ⓓ Ⓔ
6	Ⓐ Ⓑ Ⓒ Ⓓ Ⓔ	16	Ⓐ Ⓑ Ⓒ Ⓓ Ⓔ	26	Ⓐ Ⓑ Ⓒ Ⓓ Ⓔ
7	Ⓐ Ⓑ Ⓒ Ⓓ Ⓔ	17	Ⓐ Ⓑ Ⓒ Ⓓ Ⓔ	27	Ⓐ Ⓑ Ⓒ Ⓓ Ⓔ
8	Ⓐ Ⓑ Ⓒ Ⓓ Ⓔ	18	Ⓐ Ⓑ Ⓒ Ⓓ Ⓔ	28	Ⓐ Ⓑ Ⓒ Ⓓ Ⓔ
9	Ⓐ Ⓑ Ⓒ Ⓓ Ⓔ	19	Ⓐ Ⓑ Ⓒ Ⓓ Ⓔ	29	Ⓐ Ⓑ Ⓒ Ⓓ Ⓔ
10	Ⓐ Ⓑ Ⓒ Ⓓ Ⓔ	20	Ⓐ Ⓑ Ⓒ Ⓓ Ⓔ	30	Ⓐ Ⓑ Ⓒ Ⓓ Ⓔ

1. In the following figure, the shaded squares are what fractional part of the whole set of squares?

   A) $\frac{1}{2}$

   B) $\frac{5}{8}$

   C) $\frac{2}{3}$

   D) $\frac{8}{15}$

   E) $\frac{7}{15}$

2. Which of the following is greater than $\frac{14}{8}$?

   A) $\frac{1}{3}$

   B) $\frac{5}{2}$

   C) $\frac{3}{4}$

   D) 1.5

   E) 1.7

3. If $\frac{1}{3}$ of a number is greater than 9, the number must be .....

   A) Less than 9

   B) Equal to 16

   C) Equal to 27

   D) Greater than 27

   E) Equal to 36

4. If $5 \times (M + N) = 25$ and M is greater than 0, then N could Not be .....

   A) 1

   B) 2

   C) 3

   D) 4

   E) 5

5. Which of the following is closest to 6.03?

   A) 6.5

   B) 6

   C) 5.9

   D) 5.5

   E) 5.4

6. At a Zoo, the ratio of lions to tigers is 12 to 4. Which of the following could NOT be the total number of lions and tigers in the zoo?
   A) 32
   B) 64
   C) 99
   D) 104
   E) 160

7. In the multiplication bellow, A represents which digit?
$$12 \times 3A2 = 4,104$$
   A) 2
   B) 3
   C) 4
   D) 6
   E) 8

8. If M is an even number, which of the following is always an odd number?
   A) $\frac{M}{2}$
   B) $M + 40$
   C) $4M$
   D) $(2 \times M) + 2$
   E) $M + 3$

9. $9.5 - 5.08$ is closest to which of the following.
   A) 4.1
   B) 4.4
   C) 5.8
   D) 9
   E) 14

$$x = 3,564 \qquad y = 459$$

10. Numbers x and y are shown above. How many times larger is the value of digit 5 in the number x, than the value of digit 5 in the number y?
    A) 1
    B) 10
    C) 100
    D) 1,000
    E) 10,000

11. If 5 added to a number, the sum is 20. If the same number added to 35, the answer is
    A) 40
    B) 45
    C) 50
    D) 55
    E) 60

12. $\dfrac{4+5+6\times3+1}{6+2}$ =?
    A) $\dfrac{15}{8}$
    B) $\dfrac{4}{8}$
    C) $\dfrac{7}{2}$
    D) $\dfrac{6}{8}$
    E) $\dfrac{7}{4}$

13. What is the Area of the square shown below?
    A) 3
    B) 4
    C) 6
    D) 9
    E) 12

14. If 80 is the product of 20 and x, then 80 can also be divided by which of the following?
    A) $x + 5$
    B) $2x - 2$
    C) $x - 1$
    D) $x \times 4$
    E) $x + 2$

15. Use the equations below to answer the question:
$$x + 12 = 18$$
$$17 + y = 21$$

What is the value of $x + y$?

    A) 8
    B) 9
    C) 10
    D) 12
    E) 14

16. Which of the following expressions has the same value as $\frac{2}{5} \times \frac{10}{4}$?

   A) $\frac{2 \times 4}{4}$

   B) $\frac{2 \times 5}{20}$

   C) $\frac{5 \times 6}{4}$

   D) $\frac{5 \times 4}{20}$

   E) $\frac{8 \times 3}{4}$

17. When 8 is added to five times number N, the result is 83. Then N is ....

   A) 10
   B) 15
   C) 20
   D) 30
   E) 32

18. At noon, the temperature was 17 degrees. By midnight, it had dropped another 25 degrees. What was the temperature at midnight?

   A) 10 degrees above zero
   B) 10 degrees below zero
   C) 8 degrees above zero
   D) 8 degrees below zero
   E) 17 degrees below zero

19. If a triangle has a base of 6 cm and a height of 9 cm, what is the area of the triangle?

   A) $20cm^2$
   B) $27cm^2$
   C) $44cm^2$
   D) $45cm^2$
   E) $50cm^2$

20. Which formula would you use to find the area of a triangle?

   A) $length \times width \times height$

   B) $\frac{1}{2} base \times height$

   C) $length \times width$

   D) $side \times side$

   E) $\frac{1}{2}(length \times width \times heigt)$

21. What is the next number in this sequence? $3, 6, 10, 15, 21, \dots$
   A) 28
   B) 26
   C) 24
   D) 21
   E) 20

22. What is the average of the following numbers? $5, 11, 13, 23, 45$
   A) 19
   B) 19.4
   C) 19.5
   D) 20
   E) 25

23. If there are 8 red balls and 16 blue balls in a basket, what is the probability that John will pick out a red ball from the basket?
   A) $\frac{8}{16}$
   B) $\frac{1}{3}$
   C) $\frac{2}{10}$
   D) $\frac{3}{5}$
   E) $\frac{20}{10}$

24. The perimeter of a square is $60\ cm$. What is its area?
   A) $60\ cm^2$
   B) $90\ cm^2$
   C) $120\ cm^2$
   D) $225\ cm^2$
   E) $400\ cm^2$

25. What is %10 of 300?
   A) 20
   B) 30
   C) 40
   D) 50
   E) 60

26. Which of the following statement is False?
    A) $3 \times (5 - 2) = 9$
    B) $(3 + 2) \times 5 = 25$
    C) $6 \div (4 - 1) = 1$
    D) $6 \times (4 - 2) = 12$
    E) $(8 + 25) \times 10 = 330$

27. If all the sides in the following figure are of equal length and length of one side is 5, what is the perimeter of the figure?
    A) 15
    B) 18
    C) 25
    D) 30
    E) 35

28. $\frac{4}{5} - \frac{2}{5} = ?$
    A) 0.3
    B) 0.35
    C) 0.4
    D) 0.45
    E) 0.5

29. If $N = 2$ and $\frac{64}{N} + 8 = \square$, then $\square = \ldots$
    A) 30
    B) 32
    C) 34
    D) 40
    E) 44

30. Three people can paint 3 houses in 12 days. How many people are needed to paint 6 houses in 6 days?
    A) 6
    B) 8
    C) 12
    D) 16
    E) 20

End of SSAT Lower Level Math Practice Test 3

SSAT Lower Level Math Practice Test 4

2019 - 2020

Total number of questions: 30

Total time for this test: 30 Minutes

Calculator is NOT permitted for SSAT Lower Level Math Test.

SSAT Lower Level Mathematics Practice Test Answer Sheet

Remove (or photocopy) this answer sheet and use it to complete the practice test.

SSAT Lower Level Mathematics Practice Test Answer Sheet

SSAT Lower Level Practice Test 4

1	Ⓐ Ⓑ Ⓒ Ⓓ Ⓔ	11	Ⓐ Ⓑ Ⓒ Ⓓ Ⓔ	21	Ⓐ Ⓑ Ⓒ Ⓓ Ⓔ
2	Ⓐ Ⓑ Ⓒ Ⓓ Ⓔ	12	Ⓐ Ⓑ Ⓒ Ⓓ Ⓔ	22	Ⓐ Ⓑ Ⓒ Ⓓ Ⓔ
3	Ⓐ Ⓑ Ⓒ Ⓓ Ⓔ	13	Ⓐ Ⓑ Ⓒ Ⓓ Ⓔ	23	Ⓐ Ⓑ Ⓒ Ⓓ Ⓔ
4	Ⓐ Ⓑ Ⓒ Ⓓ Ⓔ	14	Ⓐ Ⓑ Ⓒ Ⓓ Ⓔ	24	Ⓐ Ⓑ Ⓒ Ⓓ Ⓔ
5	Ⓐ Ⓑ Ⓒ Ⓓ Ⓔ	15	Ⓐ Ⓑ Ⓒ Ⓓ Ⓔ	25	Ⓐ Ⓑ Ⓒ Ⓓ Ⓔ
6	Ⓐ Ⓑ Ⓒ Ⓓ Ⓔ	16	Ⓐ Ⓑ Ⓒ Ⓓ Ⓔ	26	Ⓐ Ⓑ Ⓒ Ⓓ Ⓔ
7	Ⓐ Ⓑ Ⓒ Ⓓ Ⓔ	17	Ⓐ Ⓑ Ⓒ Ⓓ Ⓔ	27	Ⓐ Ⓑ Ⓒ Ⓓ Ⓔ
8	Ⓐ Ⓑ Ⓒ Ⓓ Ⓔ	18	Ⓐ Ⓑ Ⓒ Ⓓ Ⓔ	28	Ⓐ Ⓑ Ⓒ Ⓓ Ⓔ
9	Ⓐ Ⓑ Ⓒ Ⓓ Ⓔ	19	Ⓐ Ⓑ Ⓒ Ⓓ Ⓔ	29	Ⓐ Ⓑ Ⓒ Ⓓ Ⓔ
10	Ⓐ Ⓑ Ⓒ Ⓓ Ⓔ	20	Ⓐ Ⓑ Ⓒ Ⓓ Ⓔ	30	Ⓐ Ⓑ Ⓒ Ⓓ Ⓔ

1. $\frac{8}{2} - \frac{5}{2} = ?$
   A) 0.2
   B) 0.3
   C) 0.4
   D) 1
   E) 1.5

2. If $48 = 2 \times A + 10$, then $A = \dots$
   A) 10
   B) 19
   C) 24
   D) 25
   E) 28

3. The area of each square in the following shape is $9\ cm^2$. What is the area of shaded squares?
   A) $45\ cm^2$
   B) $44 cm^2$
   C) $43 cm^2$
   D) $42 cm^2$
   E) $40 cm^2$

4. What is the value of x in the following math equation?
$$\frac{x}{15} + 8 = 12$$
   A) 15
   B) 20
   C) 45
   D) 55
   E) 60

5. When 3 is added to four times a number M, the result is 24. Which of the following equations represents this statement?
   A) $4 + 3M = 24$
   B) $24M + 4 = 3$
   C) $4M + 3 = 24$
   D) $4M + 24 = 3$
   E) $3M + 24 = 4$

6. When 105 is divided by 6, the remainder is the same as when 87 is divided by
    A) 2
    B) 4
    C) 5
    D) 8
    E) 9

7. John has 2,500 cards and Max has 505 cards. How many more cards does John have than Max?
    A) 1,995
    B) 1,898
    C) 1,812
    D) 1,728
    E) 1,704

8. In the following right triangle, what is the value of x?
    A) 15
    B) 30
    C) 45
    D) 60
    E) It cannot be determined from the information given

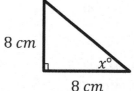

9. What is 5 percent of 450?
    A) 20
    B) 22.5
    C) 30.25
    D) 40
    E) 44.5

10. In a basket, the ratio of red marbles to blue marbles is 4 to 1. Which of the following could NOT be the total number of red and blue marbles in the basket?
    A) 15
    B) 42
    C) 55
    D) 65
    E) 70

11. A square has an area of 49 cm^2. What is its perimeter?
    A) 28 cm
    B) 30 cm
    C) 34 cm
    D) 46 cm
    E) 54 cm

12. Find the missing number in the sequence: 6, 9, 13, ..., 24
    A) 15
    B) 17
    C) 18
    D) 20
    E) 22

13. The length of a rectangle is 3 times of its width. If the length is 24, what is the perimeter of the rectangle?
    A) 24
    B) 30
    C) 56
    D) 64
    E) 66

14. Emma has y dollars. Jason has $10 more than Emma. If Jason gives Emma $13, then in terms of y, how much does Jason have now?
    A) $y + 1$
    B) $y + 10$
    C) $y - 3$
    D) $y - 1$
    E) $y + 3$

15. Dividing 207 by 6 leaves a remainder of
    A) 1
    B) 2
    C) 3
    D) 4
    E) 5

16. If $5,000 + A - 200 = 7,400$, then $A =$
    A) 200
    B) 1600
    C) 2,600
    D) 3,200
    E) 3,400

17. For what price is 15 percent off the same as $90 off?
    A) $250
    B) $300
    C) $350
    D) $450
    E) $600

18. Which of the following numbers is less than $\frac{5}{2}$?
   A) 1.07
   B) $\frac{7}{2}$
   C) 2.8
   D) 3
   E) 3.5

19. Use the equation below to answer the question.
$$x + 3 = 6$$
$$2y = 10$$
   What is the value of $y - x$?
   A) 1
   B) 2
   C) 3
   D) 4
   E) 5

20. If $320 - x + 118 = 225$, then $x =$
   A) 101
   B) 156
   C) 213
   D) 241
   E) 320

21. Of the following, 25 percent of $53.99 is closest to
   A) $9.90
   B) $10.00
   C) $13.50
   D) $14.50
   E) $15.00

22. Solve.
   $9.08 - 6.6 = ...$
   A) 2.02
   B) 2.26
   C) 2.48
   D) 3
   E) 3.2

23. If $600 + \square - 190 = 1,100$, then $\square = ?$
    A) 600
    B) 690
    C) 700
    D) 780
    E) 800

24. There are 60 students in a class. If the ratio of the number of girls to the total number of students in the class is $\frac{1}{5}$, which are the following is the number of boys in that class?
    A) 10
    B) 20
    C) 25
    D) 45
    E) 48

25. If $N \times (5 - 2) = 12$ then $N = ?$
    A) 4
    B) 12
    C) 13
    D) 14
    E) 20

26. If $x \blacksquare y = 4x + y - 2$, what is the value of $4 \blacksquare 16$?
    A) 4
    B) 28
    C) 30
    D) 36
    E) 48

27. Of the following, which number is the greatest?
    A) 0.096
    B) 0.9913
    C) 0.9923
    D) 0.9896
    E) 0.98

28. $\frac{9}{8} - \frac{3}{4} =$
    A) 0.125
    B) 0.375
    C) 0.5
    D) 0.645
    E) 0.785

29. Which of the following is the closest to 125.02?
  A) 125
  B) 125.2
  C) 1255.3
  D) 125.5
  E) 126

30. Which of the following statements is False?
  A) $(7 \times 2 + 14) \times 2 = 56$
  B) $(2 \times 5 + 4) \div 2 = 7$
  C) $3 + (3 \times 7) = 24$
  D) $4 \times (3 + 8) = 44$
  E) $14 \div (2 + 5) = 6$

End of SSAT Lower Level Math Practice Test 4

SSAT Lower Level Math Practice Test 5

2019 - 2020

Total number of questions: 30

Total time for this test: 30 Minutes

Calculator is NOT permitted for SSAT Lower Level Math Test.

SSAT Lower Level Mathematics Practice Test Answer Sheet

Remove (or photocopy) this answer sheet and use it to complete the practice test.

SSAT Lower Level Mathematics Practice Test Answer Sheet

SSAT Lower Level Practice Test 5

1	Ⓐ Ⓑ Ⓒ Ⓓ Ⓔ	11 Ⓐ Ⓑ Ⓒ Ⓓ Ⓔ	21 Ⓐ Ⓑ Ⓒ Ⓓ Ⓔ
2	Ⓐ Ⓑ Ⓒ Ⓓ Ⓔ	12 Ⓐ Ⓑ Ⓒ Ⓓ Ⓔ	22 Ⓐ Ⓑ Ⓒ Ⓓ Ⓔ
3	Ⓐ Ⓑ Ⓒ Ⓓ Ⓔ	13 Ⓐ Ⓑ Ⓒ Ⓓ Ⓔ	23 Ⓐ Ⓑ Ⓒ Ⓓ Ⓔ
4	Ⓐ Ⓑ Ⓒ Ⓓ Ⓔ	14 Ⓐ Ⓑ Ⓒ Ⓓ Ⓔ	24 Ⓐ Ⓑ Ⓒ Ⓓ Ⓔ
5	Ⓐ Ⓑ Ⓒ Ⓓ Ⓔ	15 Ⓐ Ⓑ Ⓒ Ⓓ Ⓔ	25 Ⓐ Ⓑ Ⓒ Ⓓ Ⓔ
6	Ⓐ Ⓑ Ⓒ Ⓓ Ⓔ	16 Ⓐ Ⓑ Ⓒ Ⓓ Ⓔ	26 Ⓐ Ⓑ Ⓒ Ⓓ Ⓔ
7	Ⓐ Ⓑ Ⓒ Ⓓ Ⓔ	17 Ⓐ Ⓑ Ⓒ Ⓓ Ⓔ	27 Ⓐ Ⓑ Ⓒ Ⓓ Ⓔ
8	Ⓐ Ⓑ Ⓒ Ⓓ Ⓔ	18 Ⓐ Ⓑ Ⓒ Ⓓ Ⓔ	28 Ⓐ Ⓑ Ⓒ Ⓓ Ⓔ
9	Ⓐ Ⓑ Ⓒ Ⓓ Ⓔ	19 Ⓐ Ⓑ Ⓒ Ⓓ Ⓔ	29 Ⓐ Ⓑ Ⓒ Ⓓ Ⓔ
10	Ⓐ Ⓑ Ⓒ Ⓓ Ⓔ	20 Ⓐ Ⓑ Ⓒ Ⓓ Ⓔ	30 Ⓐ Ⓑ Ⓒ Ⓓ Ⓔ

1. $\frac{8}{3} - \frac{4}{3} = ?$
   A) 0.2
   B) 0.3
   C) 0.5
   D) 0.6
   E) $1\frac{1}{3}$

2. If $58 = 3 \times N + 10$, then $N = \dots$
   A) 10
   B) 16
   C) 24
   D) 25
   E) 28

3. The area of each square in the following shape is $7\ cm^2$. What is the area of shaded squares?
   A) $35\ cm^2$
   B) $34 cm^2$
   C) $33 cm^2$
   D) $32 cm^2$
   E) $30 cm^2$

4. What is the value of x in the following math equation?
$$\frac{x}{15} + 7 = 15$$
   A) 15
   B) 20
   C) 45
   D) 105
   E) 120

5. When 3 is added to five times a number M, the result is 26. Which of the following equations represents this statement?
   A) $5 + 3M = 26$
   B) $26 \times M + 5 = 3$
   C) $5 \times M + 3 = 26$
   D) $5 \times M + 26 = 3$
   E) $3 \times M + 26 = 5$

6. When 108 is divided by 5, the remainder is the same as when 48 is divided by
   A) 2
   B) 3
   C) 5
   D) 7
   E) 9

7. Sam has 3,400 cards and Nicole has 705 cards. How many more cards does Sam have than Nicole?
   A) 2,695
   B) 2,598
   C) 2,412
   D) 2,328
   E) 2,104

8. In the following right triangle, what is the value of x?
   A) 15
   B) 30
   C) 45
   D) 60
   E) It cannot be determined from the information given

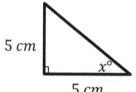

9. What is 5 percent of 360?
   A) 15
   B) 18
   C) 35
   D) 40
   E) 44.5

10. In a basket, the ratio of red marbles to blue marbles is 5 to 1. Which of the following could NOT be the total number of red and blue marbles in the basket?
    A) 18
    B) 42
    C) 55
    D) 66
    E) 72

11. A square has an area of 64 cm^2. What is its perimeter?
    A) 28 cm^2
    B) 30 cm^2
    C) 32 cm^2
    D) 46 cm^2
    E) 54 cm^2

12. Find the missing number in the sequence: $6, 9, 13, 18, \ldots \ldots, 31$
    A) 15
    B) 17
    C) 18
    D) 20
    E) 24

13. The length of a rectangle is 3 times of its width. If the length is 27, what is the perimeter of the rectangle?
    A) 24
    B) 30
    C) 66
    D) 72
    E) 76

14. Mary has y dollars. John has $11 more than Mary. If John gives Mary $13, then in terms of y, how much does John have now?
    A) $y + 1$
    B) $y + 10$
    C) $y - 2$
    D) $y - 1$
    E) $y + 2$

15. Dividing 307 by 6 leaves a remainder of
    A) 1
    B) 2
    C) 3
    D) 4
    E) 5

16. If $5,000 + A - 300 = 7,600$, then $A =$
    A) 300
    B) 2600
    C) 2,900
    D) 3,200
    E) 3,400

17. For what price is 25 percent off the same as $90 off?
    A) $250
    B) $300
    C) $360
    D) $450
    E) $500

18. Which of the following numbers is less than $\frac{7}{2}$?
    A) 2.4
    B) $\frac{9}{2}$
    C) 3.8
    D) 4.8
    E) 4.5

19. Use the equation below to answer the question.
$$x + 3 = 6$$
$$2 \times y = 10$$
What is the value of $2 \times y - 3 \times x$?
    A) 1
    B) 2
    C) 3
    D) 4
    E) 5

20. If $380 - x + 118 = 225$, then $x =$
    A) 101
    B) 256
    C) 273
    D) 291
    E) 320

21. Of the following, 25 percent of $63.99 is closest to
    A) $9.90
    B) $12.00
    C) $16.00
    D) $16.50
    E) $18.00

22. Solve.
$9.08 - 5.5 = ...$
    A) 2.42
    B) 3.46
    C) 3.58
    D) 4
    E) 4.2

23. If $700 + \square - 190 = 1{,}300$, then $\square = ?$
   A) 600
   B) 790
   C) 800
   D) 880
   E) 900

24. There are 65 students in a class. If the ratio of the number of girls to the total number of students in the class is $\frac{1}{5}$, which are the following is the number of boys in that class?
   A) 10
   B) 20
   C) 25
   D) 45
   E) 52

25. If $N \times (6 - 2) = 12$ then $N = ?$
   A) 3
   B) 12
   C) 13
   D) 14
   E) 20

26. If $x \blacksquare y = 4 \times x + y - 2$, what is the value of $5 \blacksquare 20$?
   A) 20
   B) 28
   C) 30
   D) 36
   E) 38

27. Of the following, which number if the greatest?
   A) 0.076
   B) 0.7913
   C) 0.7923
   D) 0.7896
   E) 0.78

28. $\frac{10}{8} - \frac{3}{4} =$
   A) 0.125
   B) 0.37
   C) 0.50
   D) 0.645
   E) 0.785

29. Which of the following is the closest to 7.06?

A) 7

B) 7.2

C) 7.3

D) 7.5

E) 8

30. Which of the following statements is False?

A) $(7 \times 2 + 14) \times 2 = 56$

B) $(2 \times 5 + 4) \div 2 = 7$

C) $3 + (3 \times 7) = 20$

D) $4 \times (3 + 8) = 44$

E) $14 \div (2 + 5) = 2$

End of SSAT Lower Level Math Practice Test 5

SSAT LOWER LEVEL Math Practice Tests Answer Keys

Now, it's time to review your results to see where you went wrong and what areas you need to improve.

SSAT Lower Level Math Practice Test 1				SSAT Lower Level Math Practice Test 2				SSAT Lower Level Math Practice Test 3				SSAT Lower Level Math Practice Test 4			
1	D	21	A	1	D	21	C	1	D	21	A	1	E	21	C
2	B	22	B	2	B	22	C	2	B	22	B	2	B	22	C
3	D	23	B	3	A	23	D	3	D	23	B	3	A	23	B
4	E	24	C	4	E	24	E	4	E	24	D	4	E	24	E
5	C	25	B	5	C	25	A	5	B	25	B	5	C	25	A
6	C	26	C	6	D	26	C	6	C	26	C	6	B	26	C
7	C	27	D	7	A	27	C	7	C	27	D	7	A	27	C
8	E	28	C	8	C	28	A	8	E	28	C	8	C	28	B
9	B	29	D	9	B	29	A	9	B	29	D	9	B	29	A
10	A	30	D	10	B	30	E	10	B	30	C	10	B	30	E
11	C			11	D			11	C			11	A		
12	C			12	B			12	C			12	C		
13	B			13	D			13	D			13	D		
14	D			14	C			14	D			14	C		
15	C			15	E			15	C			15	C		
16	D			16	C			16	D			16	C		
17	B			17	E			17	B			17	E		
18	D			18	A			18	D			18	A		
19	B			19	A			19	B			19	A		
20	D			20	C			20	B			20	C		

SSAT Lower Level Math Practice Test 5			
1	E	21	C
2	B	22	C
3	A	23	B
4	E	24	E
5	C	25	A
6	D	26	E
7	A	27	C
8	C	28	C
9	B	29	A
10	C	30	C
11	C		
12	E		
13	D		
14	C		
15	A		
16	C		
17	A		
18	A		
19	C		
20	C		

Score Your Test

SSAT scores are broken down by its three sections: Verbal, Quantitative (or Math), and Reading. A sum of the three sections is also reported.

For the SSAT lower level, the score range is 300-600, the lowest possible score a student can earn is 300 and the highest score is 600 for each section. A student receives 1 point for every correct answer. For SSAT Lower Level, there is no penalty for wrong answers. That means that you can calculate the raw score by adding together the number of right answers.

The total scaled score for a Lower Level SSAT is the sum of the scores for the quantitative, verbal, and reading sections. A student will also receive a percentile score of between 1-99% that compares that student's test scores with those of other test takers of same grade and gender from the past 3 years.

Use the following table to convert SSAT Lower Level Quantitative Reasoning raw score to scaled score.

SSAT Lowe Level Quantitative Reasoning raw score to scaled score

Raw Scores	Scaled Scores
Below 10	*Below* 400
11 − 15	410 − 450
16 − 20	560 − 500
21 − 25	510 − 550
26 − 30	560 − 600

SSAT Lower Level Math Practice Tests Answers and Explanations

SSAT Lower Level Quantitative Practice Test 1

1. **Choice D is correct.**

There are 10 squares and 6 of them are shaded. Therefore, 6 out of 10 or $\frac{6}{10} = \frac{3}{5}$ are shaded.

2. **Choice B is correct.**
$\frac{12}{8} = 1.5$, the only option that is greater than 1.5 is $\frac{5}{2}$. $\frac{5}{2} = 2.5$, $2.5 > 1.5$

3. **Choice D is correct.**

If $\frac{1}{3}$ of a number is greater than 8, the number must be greater than 24. $\frac{1}{3}x > 8 \rightarrow$ multiply both sides of the inequality by 3, then: $x > 24$

4. **Choice E is correct.**
$4 \times (M + N) = 20$, then $M + N = 5$. $M > 0 \rightarrow N$ could not be 5

5. **Choice C is correct.**

The closest to 5.03 is 5 in the choices provided.

6. **Choice C is correct.**
The ratio of lions to tigers is 10 to 6 or 5 to 3 at the zoo. Therefore, total number of lions and tigers must be divisible by 8. $5 + 3 = 8$. From the numbers provided, only 98 is not divisible by 8.

7. **Choice C is correct.**

A represents digit 4 in the multiplication. $14 \times 342 = 4,788$

8. **Choice E is correct.**
N is even. Let's choose 2 and 4 for N. Now, let's review the options provided.

A) $\frac{N}{2} = \frac{2}{2} = 1$, $\frac{N}{2} = \frac{4}{2} = 2$,   One result is odd and the other one is even.
B) $N + 4 = 2 + 4 = 6$, $4 + 4 = 8$ Both results are even.
C) $2N = 2 \times 2 = 4$, $4 \times 2 = 8$ Both results are even.
D) $(2 \times N) + 2 = (2 \times 2) + 2 = 6$, $(4 \times 2) + 2 = 10$ Both results are even.
E) $N + 1 = 2 + 1 = 3$, $4 + 1 = 5$ Both results are odd.

9. **Choice B is correct.**
$8.9 - 4.08 = 4.82$, which is closest to 4.8

10. **Choice A is correct.**
The value of digit 5 in both numbers x and y are in the tens place. Therefore, they have the same value.

11. **Choice C is correct.**
$5 + x = 20 \rightarrow x = 15 \rightarrow 15 + 25 = 40$

12. **Choice C is correct.**

$$\frac{2 + 5 + 6 \times 1 + 1}{5 + 3} = \frac{14}{8} = \frac{7}{4}$$

13. Choice B is correct.

Area of a square $=$ (*one side*) $\times$ (*one side*) $= 2 \times 2 = 4$

14. Choice D is correct.

$20 = x \times 4 \rightarrow x = 20 \div 4 = 5$

x equals to 5. Let's review the choices provided:

A) $x + 4 \rightarrow 5 + 4 = 9$ 20 is not divisible by 9.
B) $2x - 4 \rightarrow 2 \times 5 - 4 = 6$ 20 is not divisible by 6.
C) $x - 2 \rightarrow 5 - 2 = 3$ 20 is not divisible by 3.
D) $x \times 4 \rightarrow 5 \times 4 = 20$ 20 is divisible by 20.
E) $x + 1 \rightarrow 5 + 1 = 6$ 20 is not divisible by 6.

The answer is D.

15. Choice C is correct.

$x + 12 = 18 \rightarrow x = 6, 16 + y = 21 \rightarrow y = 5, x + y = 6 + 5 = 11$

16. Choice D is correct.

$\frac{5}{4} \times \frac{6}{2} = \frac{30}{8} = \frac{15}{4}$, Choice D is equal to $\frac{15}{4}, \frac{5 \times 3}{4} = \frac{15}{4}$

17. Choice B is correct.

$5 + 3N = 41 \rightarrow 3N = 41 - 5 = 36 \rightarrow N = 12$

18. Choice D is correct.

$15 - 20 = -5$, The temperature at midnight was 5 degrees below zero.

19. Choice B is correct.

Area of a triangle $= \frac{1}{2} \times$ (*base*) $\times$ (*height*) $= \frac{1}{2} \times 5 \times 8 = 20$

20. Choice D is correct.

area of a square $=$ *side* $\times$ *side*   *Side*

21. Choice A is correct.

$2 + 3 = 5 \rightarrow 5 + 4 = 9 \rightarrow 9 + 5 = 14 \rightarrow 14 + 6 = 20 \rightarrow 20 + 7 = 27$

22. Choice B is correct.

$$average = \frac{sum\ of\ all\ numbers}{number\ of\ numbers} = \frac{6 + 10 + 12 + 23 + 45}{5} = 19.2$$

23. Choice B is correct.

There are 8 red ball and 20 are total number of balls. Therefore, probability that John will pick out a red ball from the basket is 8 out of 20 or $\frac{8}{8+12} = \frac{8}{20} = \frac{2}{5}$.

24. Choice C is correct.

An equilateral triangle has 3 lines of symmetry.

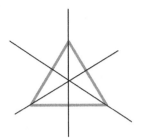

25. Choice B is correct.

10 percent of $200 = 10\%$ of $200 = \frac{10}{100} \times 200 = 20$

26. Choice C is correct.

Let's review the options provided:

A)	$2 \times 2 = 4$	This is true!
B)	$(4 + 1) \times 5 = 25$	This is true!
C)	$6 \div (3 - 1) = 1 \rightarrow 6 \div 2 = 3$	This is NOT true!
D)	$6 \times (4 - 2) = 12 \rightarrow 6 \times 2 = 12$	This is true!
E)	$(10 + 23) \times 10 = 330 \rightarrow 33 \times 10 = 330$	This is true!

27. Choice D is correct.

The shape has 6 equal sides. And is side is 4. Then, the perimeter of the shape is: $4 \times 6 = 24$

28. Choice C is correct.

$\frac{4}{5} - \frac{3}{5} = \frac{1}{5} = 0.2$

29. Choice D is correct.

$N = 2$, then: $\frac{64}{2} + 4 = 32 + 4 = 36$

30. Choice D is correct.

Four people can paint 4 houses in 10 days. It means that for painting 8 houses in 10 days we need 8 people. To paint 8 houses in 5 days, 16 people are needed.

SSAT Lower Level Quantitative Practice Test 2

1.   Choice D is correct.

$$\frac{8}{2} - \frac{3}{2} = \frac{5}{2} = 2.5$$

2.   Choice B is correct.

$48 = 3 \times N + 12 \rightarrow 3N = 48 - 12 = 36 \rightarrow N = 12$

3.   Choice A is correct.

There are 5 shaded squares. Then: $5 \times 8cm^2 = 40cm^2$

4.   Choice E is correct.

$$\frac{x}{15} + 9 = 11 \rightarrow \frac{x}{15} = 11 - 9 = 2 \rightarrow \frac{x}{15} = 2 \rightarrow x = 15 \times 2 = 30$$

5.   Choice C is correct.

$3 + (4 \times N) = 23 \rightarrow 4N + 3 = 23$

6.   Choice D is correct.
78 divided by 5, the remainder is 3. 45 divided by 7, the remainder is also 3.

7.   Choice A is correct.
$2,400 - 606 = 1,794$

8.   Choice C is correct.
All angles in a triangle sum up to 180 degrees. The triangle provided is an isosceles triangle. In an isosceles triangle, the three angles are $45, 45$, and 90 degrees. Therefore, the value of x is 45.

9.   Choice B is correct.

$$5 \ percent \ of \ 480 = \frac{5}{100} \times 480 = \frac{1}{20} \times 480 = \frac{480}{20} = 24$$

10. Choice B is correct.

The ratio of red marbles to blue marbles is 3 to 2. Therefore, the total number of marbles must be divisible by 5. $3 + 2 = 5$. 32 is the only one that is not divisible by 5.

11. Choice D is correct.

$Area \ of \ a \ square = side \times side = 81 \rightarrow side = 9$, $Perimeter \ of \ a \ square = 4 \times side = 4 \times 9 = 36$

12. Choice B is correct.

$5 + 3 = 8, \quad 8 + 4 = 12, \ 12 + 5 = 17 \ , \ 17 + 6 = 23$

13. Choice D is correct.

The length of the rectangle is 18. Then, its width is 6. $18 \div 3 = 6$, $Perimeter \ of \ a \ rectangle = 2 \times width + 2 \times length = 2 \times 6 + 2 \times 18 = 12 + 36 = 48$

14. Choice C is correct.

Mary's Money $= y$,   *John's Money* $= y + 10$, *John gives Mary* $\$12 \rightarrow y + 10 - 12 = y - 2$

15. Choice E is correct.
Dividing 107 by 6 leaves a remainder of 5.

16. Choice C is correct.
$$6{,}000 + A - 200 = 7{,}400 \rightarrow 6{,}000 + A = 7{,}400 + 200 = 7{,}600 \rightarrow A = 7{,}600 - 6{,}000 = 1{,}600$$

17. Choice E is correct.
$\$75$ off is the same as 15 percent off. Thus, 15 percent of a number is 75. Then: 15% *of* $x = 75 \rightarrow 0.15x = 75 \rightarrow x = \frac{75}{0.15} = 500$

18. Choice A is correct.

$\frac{3}{2} = 1.5 > 1.4$

19. Choice A is correct.

$x + 3 = 6 \rightarrow x = 3, 2y = 8 \rightarrow y = 4, y - x = 4 - 3 = 1$

20. Choice C is correct.
$$310 - x + 116 = 225 \rightarrow 310 - x = 225 - 116 = 109 \rightarrow x = 310 - 109 = 201$$

21. Choice C is correct.
25 percent of $\$44.00$ is $\$11$. (Remember that 25 percent is equal to one fourth)

22. Choice C is correct.
$8.08 - 5.6 = 2.48$

23. Choice D is correct.
$500 + \square - 180 = 1{,}100 \rightarrow 500 + \square = 1{,}100 + 180 = 1{,}280, \square = 1{,}280 - 500 = 780$

24. Choice E is correct.

$\frac{1}{6}$ of students are girls. Therefore, $\frac{5}{6}$ of students in the class are boys. $\frac{5}{6}$ of 60 is 50. There are 50 boys in the class. $\frac{5}{6} \times 60 = \frac{300}{6} = 50$

25. Choice A is correct.

$N \times (5 - 3) = 12 \rightarrow N \times 2 = 12 \rightarrow N = 6$

26. Choice C is correct.

If $x \blacksquare y = 3x + y - 2$, Then: $4 \blacksquare 12 = 3(4) + 12 - 2 = 12 + 12 - 2 = 22$

27. Choice C is correct.

Of the numbers provided, 0.8923 is the greatest.

28. Choice A is correct.

$\frac{7}{8} - \frac{3}{4} = \frac{7}{8} - \frac{6}{8} = \frac{1}{8} = 0.125$

29. Choice A is correct.

The closest number to 4.02 is 4.

30. Choice E is correct.

$14 \div (2 + 5) = 14 \div 7 = 2$ is not 5

SSAT Lower Level Quantitative Practice Test 3

1. Choice D is correct.

There are 15 squares and 8 of them are shaded. Therefore, 8 out of 15 or $\frac{8}{15}$ are shaded.

2. Choice B is correct.

$\frac{14}{8} = 1.75$, the only choice that is greater than 1.75 is $\frac{5}{2} \cdot \frac{5}{2} = 2.5$, $2.5 > 1.75$

3. Choice D is correct.

If $\frac{1}{3}$ of a number is greater than 9, the number must be greater than 27. $\frac{1}{3} x > 9 \rightarrow$ multiply both sides of the inequality by 3, then: $x > 27$

4. Choice E is correct.

$5 \times (M + N) = 25$, then $M + N = 5$. $M > 0 \rightarrow N$ could not be 5

5. Choice B is correct.

The closest to 6.03 is 6 in the choices provided.

6. Choice C is correct.

The ratio of lions to tigers is 12 to 4 or 3 to 1 at the zoo. Therefore, total number of lions and tigers must be divisible by 4. $3 + 1 = 4$, from the numbers provided, only 99 is not divisible by 4.

7. Choice C is correct.

A represents digit 4 in the multiplication. $12 \times 342 = 4,104$

8. Choice E is correct.

M is even. Let's choose 2 and 4 for M. Now, let's review the choices provided.

A) $\frac{M}{2} = \frac{2}{2} = 1, \frac{M}{2} = \frac{4}{2} = 2,$ One result is odd and the other one is even.

B) $M + 40 = 2 + 40 = 42, 4 + 40 = 44$ Both results are even.

C) $4M = 4 \times 2 = 8, 4 \times 4 = 16$ Both results are even.

D) $(2 \times M) + 2 = (2 \times 2) + 2 = 6, (4 \times 2) + 2 = 10$ Both results are even.

E) $M + 3 = 2 + 3 = 5, 4 + 3 = 7$ Both results are odd.

9. Choice B is correct.

$9.5 - 5.08 = 4.42$, which is closest to 4.4

10. Choice B is correct.

The value of digit 5 in number x is in the hundreds place and it is in number y in the tens place. Therefore, digit 5 in the number x, is 10 times greater than the value of digit 5 in number y.

11. Choice C is correct.

$5 + x = 20 \rightarrow x = 15 \rightarrow 15 + 35 = 50$

12. Choice C is correct.

$$\frac{4 + 5 + 6 \times 3 + 1}{6 + 2} = \frac{28}{8} = \frac{7}{2}$$

13. Choice D is correct.

Area of a square = (one side) × (one side) = $3 \times 3 = 9$

14. Choice D is correct.

$80 = x \times 20 \rightarrow x = 80 \div 20 = 4$

    x equals to 4. Let's review the choice provided:

A)	$x + 5 \rightarrow 4 + 5 = 9$	80 is not divisible by 9.
B)	$2x - 2 \rightarrow 2 \times 4 - 2 = 6$	80 is not divisible by 6.
C)	$x - 1 \rightarrow 4 - 1 = 3$	80 is not divisible by 3.
D)	$x \times 4 \rightarrow 4 \times 4 = 16$	80 is divisible by 16.
E)	$x + 2 \rightarrow 4 + 2 = 6$	80 is not divisible by 6.

The answer is B.

15. Choice C is correct.

$x + 12 = 18 \rightarrow x = 6, 17 + y = 21 \rightarrow y = 4, x + y = 6 + 4 = 10$

16. Choice D is correct.

$\frac{2}{5} \times \frac{10}{4} = \frac{20}{20} = 1$, Choice D is equal to: $\frac{5 \times 4}{20} = \frac{20}{20} = 1$

17. Choice B is correct.

$8 + 5 \times N = 83 \rightarrow 5 \times N = 83 - 8 = 75 \rightarrow N = 15$

18. Choice D is correct.

$17 - 25 = -8$, The temperature at midnight was 8 degrees below zero.

19. Choice B is correct.

Area of a triangle $= \frac{1}{2} \times (base) \times (height) = \frac{1}{2} \times 6 \times 9 = 27$

20. Choice B is correct.

area of a triangle $= \frac{1}{2} \times (base) \times (height)$

21. Choice A is correct.

    $3 + 3 = 6 \rightarrow 6 + 4 = 10 \rightarrow 10 + 5 = 15 \rightarrow 15 + 6 = 21 \rightarrow 21 + 7 = 28$

22. Choice B is correct.

$average = \dfrac{sum\ of\ all\ numbers}{number\ of\ numbers} = \dfrac{5 + 11 + 13 + 23 + 45}{5} = 19.4$

23. Choice B is correct.

There are 8 red ball and 24 are total number of balls. Therefore, probability that John will pick out a red ball from the basket is 8 out of 24 or $\frac{8}{8+16} = \frac{8}{24} = \frac{1}{3}$.

24. Choice D is correct.

The perimeter of a square is $60\ cm$. Then, one side of the square is $15\ cm$: $60 \div 4 = 15$

    Area of a square = one side × one side = $15 \times 15 = 225$

25. Choice B is correct.

10 percent of 300 = 10% of 300 $= \frac{10}{100} \times 300 = 30$

26. Choice C is correct.

Let's review the choices provided:

A) $3 \times (5 - 2) = 9$ This is true!
B) $(3 + 2) \times 5 = 25$ This is true!
C) $6 \div (4 - 1) = 1 \rightarrow 6 \div 3 = 1$ This is NOT true!
D) $6 \times (4 - 2) = 12 \rightarrow 6 \times 2 = 12$ This is true!
E) $(8 + 25) \times 10 = 330 \rightarrow 33 \times 10 = 330$ This is true!

27. Choice D is correct.

The shape has 6 equal sides. And is side is 5. Then, the perimeter of the shape is: $5 \times 6 = 30$

28. Choice C is correct.

$$\frac{4}{5} - \frac{2}{5} = \frac{2}{5} = 0.4$$

29. Choice D is correct.

$N = 2$, then: $\frac{64}{2} + 4 = 32 + 8 = 40$

30. Choice C is correct.

Three people can paint 3 houses in 12 days. It means that for painting 6 houses in 12 days we need 6 people. To paint 6 houses in 6 days, 12 people are needed.

SSAT Lower Level Quantitative Practice Test 4

1. Choice E is correct.

$$\frac{8}{2} - \frac{5}{2} = \frac{3}{2} = 1.5$$

2. Choice B is correct.

$$48 = 2 \times A + 10 \rightarrow 2 \times A = 48 - 10 = 38 \rightarrow A = 19$$

3. Choice A is correct.

There are 5 shaded squares. Then: $5 \times 9cm^2 = 45cm^2$

4. Choice E is correct.

$$\frac{x}{15} + 8 = 12 \rightarrow \frac{x}{15} = 12 - 8 = 4 \rightarrow \frac{x}{15} = 4 \rightarrow x = 15 \times 4 = 60$$

5. Choice C is correct.

$$3 + (4 \times M) = 24 \rightarrow 4M + 3 = 24$$

6. Choice B is correct.
105 divided by 6, the remainder is 3. 87 divided by 4, the remainder is also 3.

7. Choice A is correct.
$2,500 - 505 = 1,995$

8. Choice C is correct.
All angles in a triangle sum up to 180 degrees. The triangle provided is an isosceles triangle. In an isosceles triangle, the three angles are 45, 45, and 90 degrees. Therefore, the value of x is 45.

9. Choice B is correct.

$$5 \ percent \ of \ 450 = \frac{5}{100} \times 450 = \frac{1}{20} \times 450 = \frac{450}{20} = 22.5$$

10. Choice B is correct.

The ratio of red marbles to blue marbles is 4 to 1. Therefore, the total number of marbles must be divisible by 5. $4 + 1 = 5$, 42 is the only one that is not divisible by 5.

11. Choice A is correct.

$Area \ of \ a \ square \ = \ side \times side = 49 \rightarrow side = 7, Perimeter \ of \ a \ square = 4 \times \ side = 4 \times 7 = 28$

12. Choice C is correct.

$6 + 3 = 9, \quad 9 + 4 = 13, \ 13 + 5 = 18 \ , \ 18 + 6 = 24$

13. Choice D is correct.

The length of the rectangle is 24. Then, its width is 8. $24 \div 3 = 8$

$Perimeter \ of \ a \ rectangle = 2 \times width + 2 \times length = 2 \times 8 + 2 \times 24 = 16 + 48 = 64$

14. **Choice C is correct.**

$Emma's\ Money = y, Jason's\ Money = y + 10, Jason\ gives\ Emma\ \$13 \rightarrow$
$$y + 10 - 13 = y - 3$$

15. **Choice C is correct.**
Dividing 207 by 6 leaves a remainder of 3. $207 \div 6 = 34\ r3$

16. **Choice C is correct.**
   $5,000 + A - 200 = 7,400 \rightarrow 5,000 + A = 7,400 + 200 = 7,600 \rightarrow A = 7,600 - 5,000 = 2,600$

17. **Choice E is correct.**
$90 off is the same as 15 percent off. Thus, 15 percent of a number is 90.

Then: $15\%\ of\ x = 90 \rightarrow 0.15x = 90 \rightarrow x = \frac{90}{0.15} = 600$

18. **Choice A is correct.**

$\frac{5}{2} = 2.5 > 1.07$

19. **Choice B is correct.**

$x + 3 = 6 \rightarrow x = 3, 2y = 10 \rightarrow y = 5, y - x = 5 - 3 = 2$

20. **Choice C is correct.**
   $320 - x + 118 = 225 \rightarrow 320 - x = 225 - 118 = 107 \rightarrow x = 320 - 107 = 213$

21. **Choice C is correct.**
25 percent of $54.00 is $13.5. (Remember that 25 percent is equal to one fourth)

22. **Choice C is correct.**
$9.08 - 6.6 = 2.48$

23. **Choice B is correct.**
$600 + \square - 190 = 1,100 \rightarrow 600 + \square = 1,100 + 190 = 1,290, \square = 1,290 - 600\ =\ 690$

24. **Choice E is correct.**

$\frac{1}{5}$ of students are girls. Therefore, $\frac{4}{5}$ of students in the class are boys. $\frac{4}{5}$ of 60 is 48. There are 48 boys in the class. $\frac{4}{5} \times 60 = \frac{240}{5} = 48$

25. **Choice A is correct.**

$N \times (5 - 2) = 12 \rightarrow N \times 3 = 12 \rightarrow N = 4$

26. **Choice C is correct.**

If $x \blacksquare y = 4x + y - 2$, Then: $4 \blacksquare 16 = 4(4) + 16 - 2 = 16 + 16 - 2 = 30$

27. **Choice C is correct.**

Of the numbers provided, 0.9923 is the greatest.

28. **Choice B is correct.**

$$\frac{9}{8} - \frac{3}{4} = \frac{9}{8} - \frac{6}{8} = \frac{3}{8} = 0.375$$

29. Choice A is correct.

The closest number to 125.02 is 125.

30. Choice E is correct.

$14 \div (2 + 5) = 14 \div 7 = 2$ is not 6

SSAT Lower Level Quantitative Practice Test 5

1. Choice E is correct.

$$\frac{8}{3} - \frac{4}{3} = \frac{4}{3} = 1\frac{1}{3}$$

2. Choice B is correct.

$$58 = 3 \times N + 10 \rightarrow 3 \times N = 58 - 10 = 48 \rightarrow N = 16$$

3. Choice A is correct.

There are 5 shaded squares. Then: $5 \times 7cm^2 = 35cm^2$

4. Choice E is correct.

$$\frac{x}{15} + 7 = 15 \rightarrow \frac{x}{15} = 15 - 7 = 8 \rightarrow \frac{x}{15} = 8 \rightarrow x = 15 \times 8 = 120$$

5. Choice C is correct.

$$3 + (5 \times M) = 26 \rightarrow 5 \times M + 3 = 26$$

6. Choice C is correct.

108 divided by 5, the remainder is 3. 48 divided by 5, the remainder is also 3.

7. Choice A is correct.

$3,400 - 705 = 2,695$

8. Choice C is correct.

All angles in a triangle sum up to 180 degrees. The triangle provided is an isosceles triangle. In an isosceles triangle, the three angles are $45, 45$, and 90 degrees. Therefore, the value of x is 45.

9. Choice B is correct.

$$5 \, percent \, of \, 360 = \frac{5}{100} \times 360 = \frac{1}{20} \times 360 = \frac{360}{20} = 18$$

10. Choice C is correct.

The ratio of red marbles to blue marbles is 5 to 1. Therefore, the total number of marbles must be divisible by 6. $5 + 1 = 6$, 55 is the only one that is not divisible by 6.

11. Choice C is correct.

$Area \, of \, a \, square \, = \, side \times side = 64 \rightarrow side = 8, Perimeter \, of \, a \, square = 4 \times \, side = 4 \times 8 = 32$

12. Choice E is correct.

$6 + 3 = 9, \quad 9 + 4 = 13, \; 13 + 5 = 18 \; , \; 18 + 6 = 24, \quad 24 + 7 = 31$

13. Choice D is correct.

The length of the rectangle is 27. Then, its width is 9. $27 \div 3 = 9$

$Perimeter \, of \, a \, rectangle = 2 \times width + 2 \times length = 2 \times 9 + 2 \times 27 = 18 + 54 = 72$

14. Choice C is correct.

Mary's Money = y, John's Money = y + 11, John gives Mary $13 → y + 11 − 13 = y − 2

15. Choice A is correct.

Dividing 307 by 6 leaves a remainder of 1.

16. Choice C is correct.

$$5,000 + A − 300 = 7,600 → 5,000 + A = 7,600 + 300 = 7,900 → A = 7,900 − 5,000 = 2,900$$

17. Choice C is correct.

$90 off is the same as 25 percent off. Thus, 25 percent of a number is 90.

Then: $25\% \ of \ x = 90 → 0.25x = 90 → x = \frac{90}{0.25} = 360$

18. Choice A is correct.

Only choice A is less than $\frac{7}{2}$. $\frac{7}{2} = 3.5 > 2.4$.

19. Choice A is correct.

$x + 3 = 6 → x = 3, \ 2 × y = 10 → y = 5, \ 2 × y − 3 × x = 10 − 9 = 1$

20. Choice C is correct.

$$380 − x + 118 = 225 → 380 − x = 225 − 118 = 107 → x = 380 − 107 = 273$$

21. Choice C is correct.

25 percent of $64.00 is $16. (Remember that 25 percent is equal to one fourth)

22. Choice C is correct.

$9.08 − 5.5 = 3.58$

23. Choice B is correct.

$700 + □ − 190 = 1,300 → 700 + □ = 1,300 + 190 = 1,490, \ □ = 1,490 − 700 = 790$

24. Choice E is correct.

$\frac{1}{5}$ of students are girls. Therefore, $\frac{4}{5}$ of students in the class are boys. $\frac{4}{5}$ of 65 is 52. There are 52 boys in the class. $\frac{4}{5} × 65 = \frac{260}{5} = 52$

25. Choice A is correct.

$N × (6 − 2) = 12 → N × 4 = 12 → N = 3$

26. Choice E is correct.

If $x ■ y = 4 × x + y − 2$, Then: $5 ■ 20 = 4 × (5) + 20 − 2 = 20 + 20 − 2 = 38$

27. Choice C is correct.

Of the numbers provided, 0.7923 is the greatest.

28. Choice C is correct.

$$\frac{10}{8} - \frac{3}{4} = \frac{10}{8} - \frac{6}{8} = \frac{4}{8} = 0.50$$

29. Choice A is correct.

The closest number to 7.06 is 7.

30. Choice C is correct.

$3 + (3 \times 7) = 24$ is not 20

"Effortless Math" Publications

Effortless Math authors' team strives to prepare and publish the best quality Mathematics learning resources to make learning Math easier for all. We hope that our publications help you or your student Math in an effective way.

We all in Effortless Math wish you good luck and successful studies!

Effortless Math Authors

www.EffortlessMath.com

... So Much More Online!

✓ FREE Math lessons

✓ More Math learning books!

✓ Mathematics Worksheets

✓ Online Math Tutors

Need a PDF version of this book?

Please visit www.EffortlessMath.com

Made in the USA
Las Vegas, NV
15 November 2022

59567214R00044